A Note ... ...achers

DK READERS is a compelling reading programme for children. The programme is designed in conjunction with leading literacy experts, including Cliff Moon M.Ed., who has spent many years as a teacher and teacher educator specializing in reading. Cliff Moon has written more than 160 books for children and teachers. He is series editor to Collins Big Cat.

Beautiful illustrations and superb full-colour photographs combine with engaging, easy-to-read stories to offer a fresh approach to each subject in the series. Each DK READER is guaranteed to capture a child's interest while developing his or her reading skills, general knowledge, and love of reading.

The five levels of DK READERS are aimed at different reading abilities, enabling you to choose the books that are exactly right for your child:

Pre-level 1: Learning to read
Level 1: Beginning to read
Level 2: Beginning to read alone
Level 3: Reading alone
Level 4: Proficient readers

The "normal" age at which a child begins to read can be anywhere from three to eight years old. Adult participation through the lower levels is very helpful for providing encouragement, discussing storylines and sounding out unfamiliar words.

No matter which level you select, you can be sure that you are helping your child learn to read, then read to learn!

DK

LONDON, NEW YORK, MUNICH,
MELBOURNE, AND DELHI

Series Editor Deborah Lock
Designer Jemma Westing
Production Editor Sean Daly
Picture Researcher Rob Nunn
Jacket Designer Natalie Godwin
Natural History Consultant
Tom Fayle

Reading Consultant
Cliff Moon, M.Ed.

First published in Great Britain by
Dorling Kindersley Limited
80 Strand, London WC2R 0RL

Copyright © 2011 Dorling Kindersley Limited
A Penguin Company

10 9 8 7 6 5 4 3 2 1
001-182473-August 2011

A CIP catalogue record for this book
is available from the British Library

ISBN: 978-1-40537-638-9

Printed and bound in China by L Rex Printing Co., Ltd.

The publisher would like to thank the following for their kind
permission to reproduce their photographs:
a=above, b=below/bottom, c=centre, l=left, r=right, t=top

Alamy Images: The Africa Image Library 7; Guillermo Lopez
Barrera 23; Stan Gregg 30; JJM Stock Photography 20; H. Lansdown
40; Patrick Lynch 26-27; Jack Thomas 4tr; Christian Ziegler /
Danita Delimont 16. **Corbis:** Michael & Patricia Fogden 14-15;
Martin Gallagher 32-33; Steve Kaufman 21. **FLPA:** Mark Moffett /
Minden Pictures 43; Piotr Naskrecki / Minden Pictures 5crb, 7br, 17b,
38; Christian Ziegler / Minden Pictures 10-11. **Getty Images:** Gallo
Images / Travel Ink 41tr; National Geographic / Tim Laman 8-9;
Stock Illustration Source / Peter Siu 4-5; Taxi / Hans Christian Heap
37. **naturepl.com:** Mark Bowler 2, 3, 4br, 15cr; Martin Dohrn 5bl;
Kim Taylor 5tr, 12-13, 34bl; John Waters 39. **NHPA / Photoshot:**
Ken Griffiths 46-47; Dave Pinson 42; Dr. Ivan Polunin 36.
Photolibrary: Richard Packwood / Oxford Scientific (OSF) 34-35.
Science Photo Library: 23tr; Ted Clutter 31; Gregory Dimijian 19;
James H. Robinson 5tl, 28, 29. **SuperStock:** Minden Pictures 11,
17tr. **Alex Wild / myrmecos.net:** 13t, 22, 24bc, 24-25, 44, 45.
Jacket images: Front: Nature Picture Library: Meul / ARCO
All other images © Dorling Kindersley
For further information see: www.dkimages.com

Discover more at
www.dk.com

Contents

4   Ants alive!

6   Swarm raiders

14   Fungus farmers

22   Fiery team workers

30   Wood tunnellers

36   Weaving wonders

42   Speedy hunters

48   Glossary

Ant Antics

Written by Deborah Lock

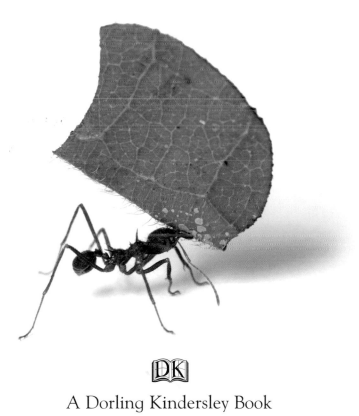

DK

A Dorling Kindersley Book

Ants alive!

Ants have been on Earth for more than 110 million years. They've spread out all over the planet and there's an estimated 10,000 trillion of them crawling around.

More than 12,000 different kinds of ants have been named and there are probably many thousands more. They survive by working together in colonies. Each tiny ant does a vital job to keep the whole colony going. Find out about the amazing busy lives of six different ants. ❖

Carpenter ants: We are found all over the world. Meet us on page 30.

Leafcutter ants: We live in Central and South America. Meet us on page 14.

Red fire ants:
We thrive all over
the world. Meet us
on page 22.

Bulldog ants: Our
colonies are mostly
found in Australia.
Meet us on page 42.

Army ants: We live
in tropical regions.
Meet us on page 6.

Weaver ants:
We live in
Africa, Asia
and Australia.
Meet us on page 36.

Swarm raiders

Get out of our way
or else!

We're army ants,
and we're always on
the hunt for food.

A colony of army ants kill more than 100,000 animals a day.

If you were a small animal in our path,
you'd have no chance against us even
if you were bigger than us.

First we'd overwhelm you with our
numbers. There are more than 200,000
of us on a raid. Then quick as a flash,
we'd cut and slice you into tiny pieces,
so that we could carry the pieces back
to our nest.

Ant senses

Ants have poor eyesight but amazing antennae to feel around and pick up smells. Ants use their antennae to find their prey, know where they are and communicate with each other.

We might be tiny, but it takes us less than 10 minutes to cut up a 5-cm (2-in) long spider and take it away to our nest, leaving nothing where the attack took place. We know our way back to the nest by following the scent trail we leave as we fan out across the forest floor.

Large soldier ants line our trail
and are ready to protect us if we are
attacked. They have much larger
mandibles (jaws) than us workers.

mandible

Back at the nest, we hand over
the pieces to the smaller workers.
They crush the pieces, squeezing
out the liquids to feed our queen,
the larvae and the rest of the colony.

Our nest is unusual. Look closely, and you'll notice it's made up of thousands of ants. When we rest we fasten on to each other, using the hooks and spines on our mandibles and on our feet. There could be more than one million ants in one colony.

Bivouacs

Army ants make living nests called bivouacs. By linking together, they form walls and tunnels, keeping their queen and her 120,000 eggs and young protected.

The site of our nest is only temporary. Once we've raided an area and can find no more food, we all move on. We mostly march at night in a long column, protected by the soldiers. We're just like an army. Some workers carry the queen and her eggs, and others carry the larvae.

Some workers go on ahead to check out the area, leaving a scent trail for the rest of us to follow.

In the daylight, we set up camp again, linking together to make a new nest.

Now we're ready to go out raiding again.

Quick!

March! ❖

Fungus farmers

Make way! We're coming through with our heavy load. These pieces of leaves might not look heavy to you, but they're five times our body weight.

We're leafcutter ants and we're all very busy. We are the harvesters, carrying the leaves to our nest. Smaller workers sit on top to stop flies from landing on the leaves.

It takes us several hours to scuttle back and forth from our nest to where the large workers are slicing off the pieces.

These workers cut
the leaves with razor-sharp
teeth on their mandibles,
which vibrate powerfully
a thousand times
per second.

*Leafcutter ants can
carry pieces at least
6 times their body weight,
which is the same as
a human carrying a small car.*

Once at the nest, we take our pieces underground and hand them over to some other workers. We don't eat the leaves but use them as compost to grow a certain type of fungus. The fungus is our food.

The underground workers grow the fungus by cutting and chewing the leaves into a gooey pulp. Like gardeners, they take great care to spread out the leaf pulp, cover it with our droppings, and then place a small piece of fungus on top.

There are millions of us in the colony and we're all sisters. Our mother, the queen ant, lays thousands of eggs every day. The younger workers look after them.

Our nest covers a large area and has several entrances. Inside, we've dug out hundreds of chambers that are about the size of a football and we grow the fungus inside them.

We have many enemies such as hunter spiders and other ants. Our large soldiers protect us from these intruders by biting them hard with their mandibles.

The small, young workers are the nurses, moving and cleaning the eggs and feeding the larvae.

As you can imagine, we create huge amounts of waste because there are so many of us. Some workers have the very important job of removing all the old fungus and waste. Like rubbish collectors, they take the waste and either bury it deep within the nest or pile it up outside. Workers on the heap move it around so that it breaks down into soil quickly.

The rest of us don't go near these workers. We don't want to catch the germs and diseases that may infect the leaves and fungus.

Well, we can't just hang around chatting. More leaves are needed. Off we go again! ❖

Fiery team workers

I wouldn't step on our nest if I were you. You don't want to upset us as we can get very, very angry. And when we're angry, we each use our lethal weapon – a poisoned stinger! We are red fire ants and we can now be found all over the world.

When we attack, we grasp our victim with our mandibles and then arch our backs under our bodies to inject venom from our stinger. We pivot on our heads and sting around in a circle. Our poison can kill small creatures and cause an extreme burning pain in humans, too.

Sting reaction

Fire ant stings cause painful swelling and blisters and burning itchiness of the skin, which needs treatment. Sometimes, people can have a life-threatening allergic reaction.

Life spans

An adult male fire ant lives for about four days after leaving the nest. A worker fire ant lives for about 180 days. A queen fire ant can live up to seven years.

Our colony was started by a young queen and a group of worker ants in just one day. She had wings back then and flew off to mate with winged male ants. Since then, our queen has been laying 1,500 eggs a day and these hatch into larvae.

The larvae change into pupae for a few weeks and later become adults. Then these young workers start looking after the queen, the eggs and the larvae, and keeping the colony clean. Our colony grows quickly. In a year, our colony had 11,000 ants and, after three years, there were 60,000 of us.

You might think we are troublemakers because we infest farmland and hurt you, but we are successful because we are organized and work together as a team.

Older workers risk danger to
go out and search for food. We eat
everything – animals and plants –
squeezing out the liquids to suck.
Working together, we can attack and
kill a lizard in less than a minute.

Many of us stay inside the nest digging out new chambers and tunnels to make room for our growing colony. Sometimes our nests have more than one queen so our colonies can have half a million ants.

To make room, we dig deeper and deeper. Some of our nests can be 1.5-m (5-ft) deep.

We push the soil up to the surface, leaving mounds more than 1-m (3-ft) high above the ground. Quite an achievement for tiny creatures! So please, don't step on us. ❖

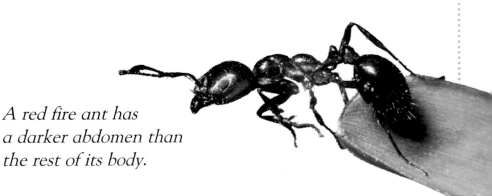

A red fire ant has a darker abdomen than the rest of its body.

Wood tunnellers

We don't eat wood. That's true!
We just use our mandibles to break
it up to make tunnels and chambers
for our nest. We are carpenter ants
and we make nests for our queen in
moist wood. Her eggs need moisture so
that they don't dry out. Most of us live
outside in rotting trees, roots and logs.

Nest sites

Indoors, the nests of carpenter ants can be found in damp or hollow places, such as around sinks, showers, and dishwashers, under roofs and in doors and walls.

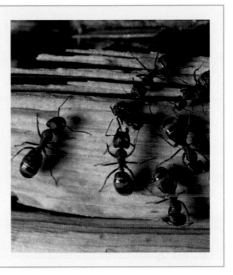

Ok, we're guilty! We do venture indoors and can do terrible damage to your homes and other buildings. Also as our colony grows, we make extra nests for just the workers and larvae in other wooden boards or beams.

As they nest and tunnel out the wood, a large colony of carpenter ants may be heard rustling or gnawing.

We're attracted into your homes by the sweet-tasting foods you have. Honey, jelly and sugar are our favourites. Outside, we find little insects called aphids, which ooze out sweet honeydew when we stroke them. We also feed on other insects, cutting them into small pieces and squeezing them for their juices.

Like all ants, we have two
stomachs – one for our own food
supply and another for food to
regurgitate (bring back up) and share
with the colony. We're most active
during the spring and summer,
going out at night to forage for
food to bring back to the nest.

In late summer, workers try to collect more food so that many of the larvae can be well fed. These well fed larvae develop into winged queen and male ants. The following spring, when the weather is warm and humid after rain, the winged ants fly from the nest. They travel far and wide. Winged ants from other nests do this at the same time.

In great swarms,
the queens mate with
the male ants.
Afterwards, the male
ants die and
the queens find
suitable damp
homes for
their new
colonies.
I expect
you're hoping
this will not
be indoors! ❖

Weaving wonders

Hold on! Pull! Nearly there! Pull! We're weaver ants and the most amazing thing about us is how we make our impressive treetop nests.

Have you ever tried sewing a bag together? Well, you take a piece of material – in our case, that's a leaf – and then fold it over, so that the edges can be sewn together. There needs to be many, many workers for us to do this.

We line up along an edge of a leaf and hold it very tightly in our mandibles. Then we begin to bend the leaf edge over towards the other edge. More workers join us, linking to our feet and helping us to pull until the edges are nearly touching.

Then, yet more workers bring larvae from our old nest and gently squeeze them. Oozing out from each larva comes a thin thread of silk. We then work on sticking the edges of the leaf together, using the silk.

Our nests can be very large, as we then begin connecting another leaf and then another. Sometimes our nests connect branches from two trees. Impressed?

We don't damage the tree. In fact, we protect it since we stop other animals from coming to live in the tree or eating parts of it.

We have many enemies that try to trick us, though. Some caterpillars produce sweet liquid called honeydew, which we love to eat. While we are distracted eating the honeydew, they crawl into the nest to eat our larvae.

Tasty snack

People in Thailand and the Philippines eat the eggs and pupae of the weaver ants. The eggs and pupae taste like lemon – juicy and a little bit sour.

Jumping spiders don't make webs but stealthily hunt for their food.

Jumping spiders smell like us, so they are able to enter our nest undetected to eat the eggs, larvae and us. It's tough being an ant! ❖

Speedy hunters

We can see you! Unlike other kinds
of ants, we have large eyes and
excellent sight. We are bulldog ants
and we are one of the largest kinds.
We are as aggressive as wasps.
In fact, scientists believe ants are
close relatives of bees and wasps.
Although we don't have wings,
we hunt and sting and live in nests
just like them.

We hunt on our own, tracking
other insects like a spy. When we
are ready, quick-as-a-flash,
we scuttle forwards to bite our victim
and bend our backs to inflict our
sting. Our stings are very powerful
and the venom acts quickly to
paralyse our prey.

Gripping tightly, we carry our victim between our long mandibles back to our nest. It can be seven times as heavy as us. The insect is chewed up and fed to the larvae. They are the meat-eaters.

Our colony only has about a 1,000 ants, so we all work hard to find enough food. When the colony is small, even our queen takes care of the eggs and her larvae, and goes out of the nest to hunt.

We all protect our nest from attack. When we are annoyed we leap around. We also chase after invaders, such as spiders and cockroaches to scare them off and get them away from our nest.

Other ants are our fiercest enemies. Although they are much smaller than we are, they can overwhelm us with their great numbers. But we don't give up easily. Even if our bodies are split in half, our heads continue to bite and our tails lash out to sting.

Like all ants, we fight for the survival of our colony, fearlessly facing death. ❖

Glossary

Allergic reaction
A very sensitive body reaction when something is eaten, touched, breathed in, or injected.

Antennae
Moveable parts on an insect's head that pick up senses.

Bivouac
An army ants' nest created by linking together their own bodies. [The term also means an army camp that is set up for a short time.]

Colony
A group of ants that live together.

Compost
A pile of rotting plants and animals that becomes fine soil that is full of nutrients.

Fungus
A plant-like living thing, such as a toadstool or mould, that does not make its own food, but lives on decaying plants and animals.

Honeydew
A sweet sticky liquid that oozes out of aphids and other small scaly insects.

Larva
The newly hatched legless form of an ant.

Mandibles
The mouthparts of an insect used for grabbing, biting, cutting, and chewing food.

Paralyse
To make an animal unable to move.

Prey
An animal hunted or captured for food.

Queen ant
A female ant that lays the eggs.

Raid
A surprise sudden attack by an army.

Regurgitate
To bring food that has been swallowed back up again into the mouth.

Soldier ant
The largest ants of the colony that protect the worker ants and defend the nest from intruders.

Stinger
A sharp-pointed tip of an ant's abdomen that can prick a victim and inject venom.

Swarm
A large number of flying insects.

Tropical
An area where the climate is hot and humid all year around.

Venom
A poisonous liquid that some ants inject into their victim by stinging.

Worker ant
The smaller ants of the colony that look after the queen, the eggs and larvae, dig out the chambers of the nest, and forage for food.